50

fantastic things to do with
squidgy stuff

KIRSTINE BEELEY & ALI

Published 2012 by Featherstone Education
Bloomsbury Publishing plc
50 Bedford Square, London, WC1B 3DP
www.bloomsbury.com

ISBN 978-1-4081-5985-9

Text © Kirstine Beeley and Alistair Bryce-Clegg 2012
Design © Lynda Murray
Photographs © Shutterstock

Printed and bound in China by C&C Offset Printing Co Ltd, Shenzhen, Guangdong
10 9 8 7 6 5 4 3 2 1

This book is produced using paper that is made from wood grown in
managed, sustainable forests. It is natural, renewable and recyclable.
The logging and manufacturing processes conform to the environmental
regulations of the country of origin.

To see our full range of titles visit www.bloomsbury.com

Acknowledgements
We would like to thank the staff and children of the following settings for their time
and patience in helping put this book together, including the use of a number of
photographs.

Acorn Childcare Ltd, Milton Keynes
Treehouse Preschool, Winslow, Bucks
Prestwood Infant School, Prestwood, Bucks
MKFocus Childcare Ltd, Milton Keynes
Penguin Preschool, Timperley, Cheshire

Also special thanks to Fee Bryce-Clegg.

Contents

Introduction

In writing this book our aim is to provide you with 50 activities that will help your children's development on a number of levels, regardless of their age. Many of the activities have been created not only to get high levels of engagement but also to develop children's experiences of texture and form. If you think that you can only squish, squash and squeeze with your hands, then you need to think again, as some of our activities involve a variety of other body parts too!

The type of experiential or 'messy' play that we have written activities for is essential for young children as it gives them endless ways to develop and learn. The great thing about messy play is that because the children have not been asked to create something specific they have the freedom to experience and try out different things. This process of evaluating success and then trying again, using what you have just found out, is an extremely powerful way of learning. Because children are discovering new things as they go along, these activities are excellent for encouraging a wide variety of language both everyday (naming familiar objects) and creative (using adjectives to describe texture, thoughts and feelings).

Children will also be experiencing lots of other concepts that are essential to their development. Most experiential play activities offer opportunities for mathematical development too as children are looking at size, shape, height and weight and using language such as bigger, smaller, longer, shorter, fatter and thinner.

Although this book is full of ideas to get children squashing and squeezing, exploring media and materials, using their imagination and responding to their experiences, the activities have also been written in an effort to foster children's interest in the world and allow them to respond to what they see, hear, smell, touch and feel.

The role of the adult is very important in these activities, because although the children need to feel like they have the time and the freedom to explore and create, they may also look to the adult for guidance and support. If when faced with a bowl of cold tapioca, you turn up your nose and squeal when you stick your hand in, you are giving a very clear message to the child about how this activity is going to turn out! So, be brave and have fun!

Skin allergy alert

Some detergents and soaps can cause skin reactions. Always be mindful of potential skin allergies when letting children mix anything with their hands and always provide facilities to wash materials off after they have been in contact with the skin. Watch out for this symbol on the relevant pages!

Food allergy alert

When using food stuffs to enhance your tactile play opportunties, always be mindful of potential food allergies. We have used this symbol on the relevant pages.

General note about using food stuffs

Some practitioners are wary of using food stuffs as part of children's play as they feel there is a moral obligation to acknowledge the lack of food in some countries around the world. Although we would not suggest using any recipe from this book with which you feel uncomfortable, some practitioners have found other ways of easing this dilemma. Why not donate an amount equal to the cost of the food used to an overseas children in need charity or maybe donate items to a local food bank? (You can find collection points at many major supermarkets now.) As well as offsetting your food use in these ways always make sure you compost as much of the used food waste wherever possible.

Messy play and parents!

Play which involves squishing and squashing materials is often referred to as 'messy play' and this label sometimes deters parents' from letting children explore the multi-sensory potential that this type of play can offer. It's important that we make parents aware of the benefits of this type of play by pointing out how squishing and squeezing can help develop children's developing pre-writing skills, as well as the endless opportunities to develop language, early science and mathematical skills.

Three bears porridge dough

What you need:

- 2 cups of plain flour
- 1 cup of salt
- 2 tablespoons of cream of tartar
- 2 cups of boiling water
- 2 tablespoons of oil
- 2 cups of porridge

What to do:

1. Mix the flour, salt and cream of tartar together.
2. Add the oil and then the water, a cup at a time and stir hard!
3. When the dough has cooled, add the oats a bit at a time.
4. Use any leftover oats to roll your dough in.

Taking it forward

- Add colour to the dough.
- Make oat dough cakes and biscuits using cake cases and cutters.
- Link the dough to the 'Goldilocks and the three bears' story to encourage discussion and role-play.

What's in it for the children?

Children will have opportunities to explore the textural differences in the ingredients being used. You can use this activity to make lots of links to well-known stories that are familiar to them. Children will have opportunities for the development of 'story language' as well as descriptive language.

Top tip ⭐

Too many oats in your mixture will make your dough too dry and crumbly so add them slowly.

Bags of fun

What you need:

- Zip lock freezer bag
- Cold water
- Food colouring
- Vegetable oil
- Golden syrup

What to do:

1. Mix some food colouring with water in a pot.
2. Put 4 tablespoons of vegetable oil into the bottom of your plastic bag.
3. Then add 4 tablespoons of coloured water.
4. **WAIT** (and see what happens).
5. Add 4 tablespoons of golden syrup to the bag.
6. **WAIT.**
7. Zip up the bag and let the children squish!

Taking it forward

- Ask the children if they think it will make a difference if the liquids are added in a different order.
- Start with some small objects in the bag (plastic bugs, jewels) and see where they end up.
- Drop some small objects in just before you seal the bag. Where do they end up?

What's in it for the children?

Apart from all of the language involved in creating the bag, children will have the opportunity to explore the textures of all of the liquids before they go into the bag. They will have opportunities to develop their prediction skills and begin to explore the concept that heavier liquids sink and that oil and water do not mix.

Top tip ⭐

When adding the golden syrup use a warm spoon (stand it in a cup of hot water first) then the syrup will just glide off.

Frost fingers

What you need:

- Clear glass plate
- Petroleum jelly
- Freezer

What to do:

1. Cover the glass plate in a fairly thick layer of petroleum jelly.
2. Use fingers to draw a design into the jelly.
3. Put into the freezer for at least 2 hours.
4. Touch and feel your frosty design until it has melted again.

Taking it forward

- Use a mirror for a reflective frosty picture.
- Add a sprinkling of glitter before you freeze for extra sparkle.
- Create a petroleum jelly mound, pushing in your finger to make a hole and filling with water before freezing.

What's in it for the children?

Children will get the opportunity to experience the very slippery texture of petroleum jelly. They will also be able to observe how the jelly changes when it has been in the freezer. This activity provides lots of opportunities for descriptive language development.

Top tip ★

This turns into a VERY greasy activity so have plenty of wipes on hand.

Bread dough

What you need:

- **450g strong white bread flour**
- **1 tsp salt**
- **2tsp dried easy blend yeast**
- **300ml water** (that has been boiled)
- **2 tablespoons of oil**

Taking it forward

- Experiment with different sizes and shapes of bread.
- Add things to your dough like herbs or chocolate chips.
- Colour the dough and make green, black or purple bread.
- Experiment with adding other toppings to your bread such as poppy seeds, cheese or porridge oats (ALWAYS check for allergies).

What's in it for the children?

This activity gives children a much better understanding of how their food is made. You could replace the standard measures with non-standard measures to make the process simpler for the children. The act of kneading the bread is good for upper body muscle development.

Top tip ★

Allow plenty of time for this activity as there is lots of 'waiting' for the bread to rise.

What to do:

1. Sift flour and salt into a bowl and then add yeast.

2. Slowly stir in the warm water and oil with a wooden spoon to make a dough.

3. Put the dough onto a clean surface and knead thoroughly for about 10 minutes.

4. Put the dough into a large clean bowl, cover with food wrap and leave in a warm place for an hour and a half.

5. Tip out the dough (it should be at least twice the size by now) and knead again for a couple of minutes.

6. Separate into individual pieces and roll into small balls (about the size of a ping pong ball).

7. Heat your oven to 220C, gas mark 7.

8. Place on a greased tray and leave in a warm place for 40 minutes to rise.

9. Brush a little milk over the top of your rolls.

10. Bake for 10-12 minutes.

Cereal crunching

What you need:

- **Breakfast cereal such as puffed rice, cornflakes etc.**
- **Large bowl** (washing-up bowl size)

What to do:

1. Get the children to pour the dry cereal into the washing up bowl, watching how it moves and listening to the sound it makes.

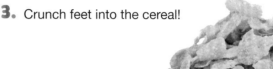

2. Take off shoes and socks.
3. Crunch feet into the cereal!

Taking it forward

- Put the bowl or tray onto the table and use hands to try and catch the cereal as it is being poured.

- Squeeze and crunch the cereal in the palms of your hands.

- Use fingers to 'walk' through the cereal and crunch it.

- Make tight fists and crunch the cereal with your knuckles.

- Scoop and pour the cereal with hands or different sized spoons.

What's in it for the children?

Children have the opportunity to experience the texture of the dry cereal in a number of ways. Using dry material is also a really good introduction to the concept of pouring as it is much easier to control than liquid. Pouring dry ingredients over the hands encourages very young children to open them.

Top tip ⭐

Puffed rice cereals work well; sugar coated 'flakes' can be sharp so watch out!

Edible finger paints

What you need:

- 2 cups of cornflour
- 1 cup of cold water
- 4½ cups of boiling water
- Food colouring

What to do:

1. Mix the cornflour with the cold water and stir together.

2. Pour in the boiling water and stir between each cup.

3. **KEEP STIRRING!**

4. When it becomes like the consistency of thick custard it's done.

5. Either separate into smaller containers and add food colouring if you are making more than one colour or add food colouring to the pan for one colour.

Health & Safety

Pouring and mixing the boiling water is an adult only part of the activity

Taking it forward

- Try adding sand or sawdust to the cooled paint to give more texture.

- Add flavouring or scented oils for an extra sensory dimension.

- Let the children apply it direct to the tabletop and then take a relief print of their work.

- Put the paint into plastic bags, seal the top and then snip off one corner. The children can then 'pipe' the paint onto their chosen surface.

What's in it for the children?

Children get a great deal of satisfaction from making their own paint and are keen to get involved. The mixing of the ingredients allows the children to observe lots of changes in the mixture and also gives extensive opportunities for the introduction/use of descriptive language. Encouraging the children to spread the paint widely across a tabletop or vertical surface is good for developing their upper body movement and hand/eye coordination.

Top tip ⭐

If you want a 'bold' colour you need to add lots of food colouring. If the children spread the paint on thickly it will take a while to dry.

What you need:

- Shampoo or washing-up liquid
- Water or a rainy day!
- Stiff outdoor brushes

What to do:

1. Pour shampoo or washing-up liquid onto the ground outside.
2. Add some water.
3. Let the children brush to make suds.

Health & Safety

The floor can get very slippy so adult supervision is needed at all times!

Taking it forward

- You could do a similar activity but in a tuff tray.

- You can add a few drops of food colouring to give you rainbow suds.

- Add a dash of oil for an even more slippery experience.

- Put the tuff tray on the floor and let children mix with their feet.

- You could add some glitter or sequins to the suds – beware children rubbing their eyes with glittery fingers.

What's in it for the children?

Mixing the shampoo and the water together with big movements is great for developing children's' gross motor coordination and upper body muscles. Using feet as well as/instead of hands gives an opportunity to experience texture using another part of the body.

Top tip ⭐

Add pan scrubs, sponges, nail brushes etc for an extra dimension.

Fruit putty

What you need:

- 1 packet of crystalised or powdered jelly
- 2 cups of flour
- 1 cup of salt
- 4 tbsp cream of tartar
- 2tbs cooking oil
- 2 cups of boiling water
- A pan
- Somewhere to heat the pan

Taking it forward

- Use different flavours of jelly to get different colours and scents.
- Add food colouring with the water for a more intense colour.
- Add less water and two tbsp of oil for a thicker more stretchy dough.

What's in it for the children?

You can ask the children to predict what they think is going to happen when you add the jelly to the mixture. Try covering the jelly packet and ask the children if they can identify the flavour of the jelly first by smell, then by taste, then by colour. Using a thicker mix of dough will really challenge children to use more arm and hand strength to manipulate it.

What to do:

1. Mix all of the dry ingredients together in a pan.
2. Add the boiling water and stir.
3. Heat the pan and keep stirring until the ingredients come together to form a ball.

Top tip ★

This is great to stick your hands into while it is still warm - NB: check it's not still too hot on the inside even if the outside has cooled.

Hair gel squishy bags

What you need:

- **1 tube of cheap clear hair gel**
- **Thick zip lock freezer bags**
- **Food colouring** (cake maker's colouring is more vivid)

What to do:

1. Squirt some gel into a pot.
2. Add food colouring.
3. Mix thoroughly.
4. Spoon into zip-lock bag.
5. Seal. You can add additional tape along the sealed edge if you want to be really sure.

Taking it forward

- Lay photographs or numbers under the bag for the children to trace.
- Add glitter to your gel.
- Use lolly sticks to move the gel around and make patterns.
- Put your bags in the fridge/ freezer to change the texture and experience.
- Put small items inside the bag for the children to find or move around.
- Put the bags into your water tray for an extra sensory dimension.

What's in it for the children?

By squeezing their bag the children get to practise and develop their fine and gross motor manipulation. The feeling of the gel in the bag is great for language development. As well as developing pre-writing skills, you could also use this activity to impact on colour recognition, shape recognition… the list is endless depending on what you put under or in your bag!

Top tip ⭐

Don't overfill your bag or it will burst. A little goes a long way!

Get stuck in!

What you need:

- Sticky-backed plastic
- A table
- Masking tape
- A variety of interesting objects

What to do:

1. Cover your table in sticky-backed plastic with the sticky side UP!

2. Stick the edges of the plastic to the table with masking tape.

3. Scatter a few items across the tabletop to give children the idea.

4. Let the children self select what they would like to stick – including themselves!

Taking it forward

- Have a number of items of various textures available for the children to experiment with.

- Introduce small-wheeled toys (such as cars) for the children to use.

- Get the children to talk about and imagine where a sticky table like this could be useful.

What's in it for the children?

The children get to practise lots of muscle work with their hands and fingers. By doing this activity they gain opportunities to experiment and hypothesise about possible outcomes. They also get the chance to explore a range of textures and have direct experience of cause and effect.

Top tip ⭐

Leave the backing on your sticky-back plastic. Peel it up a little way on one side of the table and attach with masking tape, then peel off the backing and secure at the other side. The tighter the plastic, the better the effect.

Tapioca

What you need:

- 1 packet of dry tapioca
- Warm water
- Food colouring
- Flavouring/scented oils (optional)

What to do:

1. Boil the tapioca with water following the instructions on the packet.
2. Add food colouring.
3. Add flavouring.

FOOD allergy!

Health & Safety

For safety reasons this recipe must be prepared by adults.

Taking it forward

Let the children experience the tapioca before it is cooked.

Put the cooked tapioca in a tuff tray or your sand/water tray.

Hide objects under a 'sea' of tapioca to be retrieved.

Let the children experience it both warm and cold.

What's in it for the children?

There are lots of opportunities for language development. This activity is great for experiencing differences in texture when things are dry and then wet. Using taste and texture in the mouth gives a whole added dimension to the experience.

Top tip ★

Let the children try eating tapioca made with milk. It is a great squash and squeeze experience in their mouths.

Squeezable clouds of soap

What you need:

- **1 bar of white soap** (Ivory soap is a good brand to use for this activity as it is whipped during production which makes it super bubbly)
- **Microwave**
- **Kitchen towel**

What to do:

1. Put a bar of soap onto a couple of pieces of kitchen towel in the microwave.

2. Heat on full power for 2 minutes – then check for movement.

3. Continue to heat on full power for a minute at a time.

4. When the soap has grown into a **HUGE** cloud remove from the microwave.

5. Your cloud is now ready to be squeezed!

Health & Safety

Never let children handle materials straight from a microwave. Allow to cool first.

Taking it forward

- Try different types of soap.
- Cut the soap into smaller chunks before you microwave to get smaller clouds.
- Send each child home with a cloud of soap for their bath.

What's in it for the children?

Children will get opportunities to see changing materials. Before they touch it, get them to try and predict what the cloud might feel like (it is actually quite firm).

Because of its unique texture there are lots of opportunities for descriptive language development.

Top tip ⭐

Make sure your microwave is on a level that children can see the changes happen through the door.

squeezy puffy paint

What you need:

- I cup of grated soap (white)
- ¾ cup of warm water
- Food colouring
- Zip lock freezer bag

What to do:

1. **SLOWLY** add the water to the grated soap.
2. Stir gently otherwise you will get bubbles – you are aiming for a thick paste.
3. Spoon the paste into zip lock bags.
4. Add a few drops of food colouring to each bag and let the children squash until it's mixed in!
5. Snip the corner off the bag and squeeze away (always start with a small snip – you can always make it bigger if you need to).
6. Make patterns with your puffy paint.

Taking it forward

- As this is made from soap, try painting the inside of your water tray before you add the water and then making coloured lather.
- Once all of the bags are empty, let the children mix the colours together and experiment with the texture.
- You can mix in glitter for that extra bit of shimmer.

What's in it for the children?

There are lots of opportunities to observe changing materials. This is also a good activity for developing fine motor control in squeezing the bag and directing the paint. There are opportunities to develop children's use of instructional language around the making of the paint and then descriptive language in relation to the texture of it.

Top tip ★

If you are only making one colour, add your food colouring to the water before you add it to the soap.

Pink slime

What you need:

- 1 bag of marshmallows (pink)
- Washing up-liquid
- A pan

What to do:

1. Heat the marshmallows in the pan until they begin to melt and become sticky (be careful not to overheat and burn).

2. Add a good squirt of washing-up liquid to make the marshmallows sticky and slimy.

FOOD allergy!

Taking it forward

- Use white marshmallows and add food colouring to create a range of sticky coloured slime.

- Put into a thick clear plastic freezer bag, seal the top and then snip off one corner so that the children can 'pipe' out their slime.

- The 'slime' can be used for creating pictures, but it takes a long time to dry!

What's in it for the children?

There are lots of opportunities for language development. This activity is also great for experiencing changes in materials as the marshmallows melt. It makes children's hands very sticky so is useful for exploring that sensation.

Top tip ⭐

You can use a microwave instead of a pan but never let children handle food straight from a microwave.

Rainbow gloop

What you need:

- 2 cups of cornflour
- 1 cup of water
- Food colouring (various)

What to do:

1. Mix the cornflour and water together (aim for a fairly thick consistency).
2. Spread the gloop onto a table top or tray.
3. Dot food colouring onto the gloop in various places.
4. Drag your fingers through the gloop to move and mix the colours.

Taking it forward

- You can add other things to the gloop such as glitter, sequins, and plastic spiders!
- Encourage the children to use all of their fingers singly and at the same time.
- Take a relief print of the patterns they create.
- Pour the gloop onto tin foil or shiny coloured paper to get a different effect.

What's in it for the children?

This is a great activity for children to develop fine motor skills. Encourage children to really use their imagination and tell you what they can see hidden within the patterns they create. You can use the technique to make interesting and unusual habitats for small world play.

Top tip ★

Let the children experiment with the gloop mixture to see what happens when they use different amounts of ingredients.

Porridge goo

What you need:

- Porridge oats
- Warm water
- Food colouring/powder paint
- Large tray

What to do:

1. Put the dry oats into a large tray and let the children experience, touch and play with them.

2. Add warm water a little at a time and get the children to mix it in with their fingers.

3. Add food colouring or powder paint to different parts of the tray and mix with fingers.

Taking it forward

- Change the texture of the porridge by cooking it in a pan until really thick. Make sure it has cooled then pour into a tray and squish.

- Mix dry porridge and water to make a 'soup' and then leave it overnight to see what happens.

- Hide objects in cooled cooked porridge for children to discover – you could colour it green and create a porridge swamp.

- Use your porridge 'goo' to create small world environments. Let your pigs and hippos wallow in a porridge mud pool.

Top tip ⭐

If your porridge starts to get too sticky, add a squirt of washing up liquid to change its texture.

Great activity for children to observe change. The texture of the porridge gives lots of opportunities for developing children's talk and language.

Sand dough

What you need:

- 2 cups of plain flour
- 1 cup of salt
- 2 tablespoons of cream of tartar
- 2 tablespoons of oil
- 2 cups of boiling water
- 2 cups of sand
- Few drops of yellow food colouring

Taking it forward

- Use this sand dough for beach role-play or small world play.
- Mold the dough into different sized containers to make big and little sandcastles.
- Use other tactile objects like ridged shells or smooth glass beads to decorate your sand dough structures.

What's in it for the children?

This activity is a good one for strengthening hand muscles for fine motor development. There is lots of scope for using this dough in imaginative play and creativity. The mix of textures provides lots of opportunities for developing language and vocabulary not to mention knowledge and understanding of the world, relating to the beach and seaside.

Top tip ⭐

This will keep for a long time if you store it in a sealed container.

What to do:

1. Mix the flour, salt and cream of tartar together.
2. Put the food colouring and oil in the water and add a cup at a time and stir hard!
3. Add the sand a bit at a time.

Sand mousse

What you need:

- Play sand
- Water
- Washing-up liquid

What to do:

1. Make a well in the middle of your sand.
2. Slowly pour in your water.
3. Add a squirt of washing-up liquid.

SKIN allergy !

The quantities depend on how much mousse you want. Half of the fun is adding different amounts of the ingredients as you go along to get the desired effect.

Taking it forward

- Add food colouring to make sand mousse of different shades.

- Make a large amount and use it as part of your outdoor exploratory or small world play.

- This makes a great substitute for real cement if you are role-playing bricklaying.

What's in it for the children?

Sand mousse has a real gritty whilst slippery texture so can offer another dimension to children's exploratory play. This is an easy one for children to make themselves. They will often spend as long working on their perfect recipe as they do playing with it.

Top tip ★

Although not a problem when the sand mousse is fresh, it will begin to smell after a couple of days – so beware!

Slippery, squidgy balloons

What you need:

- A packet of balloons
- Water
- Baby oil
- Tuff tray or sand tray

What to do:

1. Fill different balloons with different amounts of water.
2. Blow in a small amount of air.
3. Tie the balloon.
4. Put into a tuff tray or sand tray with a good squirt of baby oil.
5. Try and squeeze the balloons and then catch them.

Taking it forward

- Fill balloons with different substances for different effects. You could use sand, lentils, and cooked porridge.
- Make some balloons hard with extra air as this gives a higher level of challenge to the catcher.
- Introduce a sand timer and turn the activity into a game.

What's in it for the children?

Children will be using lots of skills to watch, stop and catch the balloons. They will be developing their hand/eye coordination as well as their gross motor arm movement and grabbing as well as fine motor pincer grip.

Top tip ⭐

Blow into the balloons a couple of times before you fill them.

Soap flake pancake

What you need:

- 1 box of soap flakes
- Water
- Tray for exploring

What to do:

1. Add water to your soap flakes and stir gently until you have the consistency of double cream.

SKIN allergy!

2. Pour into a tray (or frying pan) and leave to set. (How long this process takes depends on how thick your pancake is).

3. Turn out your rubbery pancake into your tray and begin to explore.

Taking it forward

- When the pancake begins to break up add some warm water to the tray.

- As the tray gets soapier add other things to mix and scrub with.

- Provide straws, sticks and other pattern making implements.

- Try adding spots of food colouring or powder paint and mixing it in.

What's in it for the children?

Lots of opportunities for fine and gross motor manipulation. Because this is such a tactile activity there is lots of scope for creative language development. Children also have the opportunity to observe changing materials. If you added drops of food colouring to your 'pancake' you could even look at colour mixing and pattern while you squished!

Top tip ★

This activity starts fairly dry and then gets VERY wet so be prepared!

Soapy snow

What you need:

- **Soap flakes**
- **Water**
- **Whisk** (either electric or hand)

What to do:

1. Add soap flakes to the water a little at a time.
2. Get the children to whisk the water.
3. Have fun with your mountains of snowy bubbles.

SKIN allergy !

Taking it forward

- Use a smaller amount of water for thicker 'snow' which can be modeled and moulded.
- Provide a range of whisks in a number of sizes to encourage the children to create their own snow.
- Drop food colouring into the foamy snow and use fingers to swirl it and make patterns.

What's in it for the children?

The mixing and whisking action is good for developing children's upper body control. If you mix 'thick snow' it will encourage the children to use their fingers and hands to improve coordination and grip. Watching the soap flakes dissolve in the water and then change into foam allows the children to observe change at first hand.

Top tip ⭐

Strong soap solution can really dry the skin so make sure the children wash their hands thoroughly after this one.

Sparkly cloud dough

What you need:

- 5 cups of plain flour
- 1 cup of baby oil
- Bowl for mixing
- Glitter (optional)
- Food colouring (optional)

What to do:

1. Stir the oil into the flour.
2. Add the glitter and/or food colouring.

Taking it forward

- Use different-sized and shaped pots to mould the dough.
- Add flavouring or scented oil for an added sensory dimension.

What's in it for the children?

There is a great contrast between the dryness of the flour and the slipperiness of the oil. The squeezing of the dough to mould it is a good way to develop children's grip and fine motor skills. Also, the range of things that children can create allows them to explore model making and imaginative play. This activity makes a great addition to any exploratory area indoors or out.

Top tip ★

The dough will stay 'fresh' for a couple of weeks if stored in an airtight container.

Jelly

What you need:

- Jelly cubes or crystals
- Warm water
- Different-sized plastic containers/moulds
- Ice cube tray
- Rubber/plastic gloves
- Plastic bags
- A selection of small interesting objects (jewels, creepy crawlies)

What to do:

1. Mix up your jelly as per the instructions on the packet.

2. Pour into a number of different-sized containers.
3. You could use a plastic glove for a jelly handshake! (You will have to cut the glove off once the jelly has set.)
4. For a different sensory experience, pour some liquid jelly into a sealable plastic bag.
5. Add any other 'objects' to your jelly at the liquid stage.
6. When the jelly is set, let the children tip it out of the moulds onto a large surface and get stuck in.

Taking it forward

- Try putting the jelly into a bowl and letting the children mash it with their feet.
- Use the jelly to create exciting habitats for animals in small world play.
- Let the children squish the jelly from outside of the bag. Does it feel different?
- Can the children think of a way to turn the set jelly back into liquid?

Top tip ⭐

If you are using jelly play to help strengthen and develop children's fine motor skills then mix it with much less water than recommended. This will give you a more runny substance to work with.

What's in it for the children?

Jelly play encourages children to manipulate and mould materials. There are lots of opportunities for language development as well as opportunities to encourage children's fine motor skills. Depending on the range of jellies and containers available, you can introduce children to a variety of different smells, colours and shapes.

White bread and glue dough

What you need:

- 1 slice of white bread (no crusts)
- 1 tablespoon of PVA glue
- Small bowl

What to do:

1. Tear bread into tiny pieces and put into the bowl.
2. Add the glue.
3. Get squidging with your fingers.
4. Keep going until you have a sticky dough-like consistency.

Taking it forward

- Try adding some food colouring to the glue.
- Use hands and fingers to roll the dough into balls.
- Make on a much larger scale and use for model making.
- Mix with flour and water paste instead of PVA and leave models out for the birds.

What's in it for the children?

The children get to consolidate and extend their fine motor manipulation with the tearing of the bread and kneading in the glue. They can also observe changes in materials and texture from the dry bread to the wet glue. There are also many opportunities for the development of their sequential and descriptive language.

Top tip ⭐

If the dough gets too dry, add more glue or a TINY drop of water. If it gets too sticky just add more bread. It will dry very quickly but you can keep it moist in an airtight container.

Witches' brew

What you need:

- Plastic pots/containers
- Clear vinegar
- Food colouring
- Glitter
- Washing up liquid
- Bicarbonate of soda

What to do:

1. Half fill a container with vinegar.
2. Add several drops of food colouring.
3. Sprinkle glitter over the top of the vinegar.
4. Add a squeeze of washing-up liquid.
5. Gently mix together.
6. Add a heaped teaspoon of bicarbonate of soda to the liquid.
7. Watch what happens!
8. Dip your fingers in the froth.

SKIN allergy!

Taking it forward

- Mix two or more food colours together and get colour mixing froth!
- Add different amounts of bicarbonate of soda to see what happens.

What's in it for the children?

You can link this activity to a book, song or poem. Encourage children to think about why the liquid starts to foam. Running their fingers through the foam is a good introduction to light, frothy textures. You can link this activity to a number of stories and poems, providing lots of opportunities for language development.

Top tip ★

Add more washing-up liquid or some soap flakes for even frothier foam!

All wrapped up

What you need:

- **Flat table top surface** (not two tables pushed together as this won't work!)
- **Ready mixed paints in a variety of colours**
- **Roll of cling film** (extra long probably better as you will need quite a lot)

Taking it forward:

- Use shaving foam mixed with paint or food colouring instead of just paint.
- Add glitter to your paint mix before cling filming the table.
- Try a mixture of coloured baby oil or hair gel instead of paint.
- Use the same mixes above in small clear zip wallets or sealable food bags for individual exploration and squishy mark making.

What's in it for the children?

This activity combines all the sensory wonders of messy play with great mark making and has the added advantage of appealing to those children who do not like getting messy.

Top tip ★

Food colouring and paints can colour table surfaces if left on too long - try smearing the table top with baby oil prior to adding paints to make it easier to wipe off.

What to do:

1. Squirt blobs and trails of different coloured ready mixed paints directly onto the table top towards the centre. (Be quite generous as you can't add more later – better too much than not enough!)

2. Lay the cling film the entire length of the table, roll it under the table and up the other side, continuing to wrap the entire table top until it is completely sealed with the film (check that table edges and table legs are sealed too – you can use tape if you need to).

3. Allow children to push and squish the paint around the surface under the film.

4. Explore mixing the colours and making marks in the paint with your fingers.

Health & Safety

Always dispose of the cling film straight away after removal so that it does not pose a suffocation hazard.

What you need:

- **A wide selection of dried beans, peas and pulses in a variety of sizes and colours.** Include: split peas, black eye peas, cannelloni beans, butter beans, red lentils, green lentils, pearl barley but don't use kidney beans as these can be toxic when uncooked.

- **Trays**

- **Scoops, spoons, pots and pans** (plastic and metal)

- **Sieves**

What to do:

1. Pour the beans, peas and pulses onto a tray and explore using fingers and the scoops, spoons, pots, pans and sieves.

2. Encourage children to see which pulses go through different sized sieves.

3. Pour pulses and beans into the pots and pans, what noise do different pots make?

Taking it forward:

Explore other dried foods including pasta (page 47), cereals (page 10).

Use some more pulses and beans etc to cook a bean soup and explore how they change when they have been cooked. (Don't cook with the pulses you have been playing with!)

Try exploring baked beans – do they feel different? (see page 36)

Make shapes and patterns in the pulses on the tray... try on a mirror or a light box.

Top tip ⭐

After use, the beans can be sealed in an airtight container and saved for another day.

What's in it for the children?

A colourful, natural resource which offers children lots of opportunities to explore size, shape and colour as well as mark making in a fun way. If you cook the pulses and beans you will have lots of opportunities to discuss changes and to develop early science language.

Buckets full of beans

What you need:

- **Tinned baked beans** (catering tins are cheaper)
- **Big shallow trays** (sand/water tray ideal)
- **Buckets, scoops, spoons** (wooden and metal)**, sieves and colanders**

What to do:

1. Pour enough baked beans into the tray so that children are able to pour and scoop up lots of beans and sauce at the same time.

FOOD allergy!

2. Allow children to explore playing with the mixture.

3. Include sieves and colanders so children are able to separate the beans from the mixture.

Taking it forward

- Add other types of tinned beans to the mixture (different sizes such as butter beans will allow for exploration of language about sizes).

- Use dark food colouring to change the mixture (black has a dramatic effect).

- Add some plastic crocodiles and some small twigs with leaves to create your own baked bean swamp!

What's in it for the children?

This is a great activity for exploring the properties of familiar materials as well as exploring the use of tools such as sieves, scoops etc. It's great for children to explore familiar materials in unfamiliar situations.... early science exploration at its best!

A chip off the old block!

What you need:

- **A pack of new sealed pet bedding sawdust** (this tends to have smaller pieces and less chance of splinters)

- **A tray – cat litter tray or sand/water tray**

- **Scoops, spoons, pots, sieves, sand wheels, etc**

- **Water**

What to do:

1. Pour sawdust into the tray.

2. Enjoy and explore using the tools, wheels, scoops and spoons, as you would with sand play.

3. Once children are used to playing with the dry sawdust allow them to add water and mix and explore all over again.

Handy hint

Dispose of the sawdust after use – recycle by digging it into a garden if at all possible.

aking it forward

Add sequins or shaped foil confetti for a bit of sparkly fun.

Hide treasure in the dry sawdust and see if children can sieve it out or give them a treasure map and list of treasure to dig up.

Try and make wet 'sawdust castles'. Are they as good as sandcastles?

Paint with PVA glue and sprinkle sawdust on to make woody patterns in the same way as you would with glitter.

Add safari animals as a starting point for imaginative play and talk.

hat's in it for the children?

the same way that sand play
lows children the opportunity
build on skills for pouring and
gging, sawdust gives them the
ance to revisit many of these skills.
e contrast between wet and dry
awdust in both texture and the way
ey behave, are good early starting
pints for science discussions.

Clay

What you need:

- **Shallow tray** – builders' tray is ideal (gardening gravel tray provides a smaller alternative)
- **Tarpaulin to cover the floor**
- **Clay**
- **Water**
- **A selection of tools** (sticks, spoons, brushes, etc)

What to do:

1. Place the tray on the floor on top of the tarpaulin (either indoors or outdoors).

2. Put a really big lump of clay into the tray (the bigger the better) – at least 20cm wide.

3. Encourage children to lean in and squish their fingers into the clay, pulling and squashing the clay block.

4. Add water a little at a time and continue to explore the increasingly sticky and slimy mix.

5. Explore the clay with sticks, spoons, brushes etc making patterns and shapes in the soft mixture, as well and pulling off pieces and rolling in hands, pulling and squashing.

6. If you use air hardening clay you can leave bits of the clay out and explore it again as it hardens.

Taking it forward

■ Paint with clay – mix with lots of water to make a thick mixture and paint onto paper or natural materials such as leaves, sticks or conkers.

■ Use clay instead of play dough to explore making, rolling and cutting.

■ Add natural materials to your clay mix and explore using your senses (include pebbles, fir cones etc.)

■ Make tree faces by pushing clay onto a tree trunk and adding leaves, twigs, stones etc to make the facial features. (The materials dry over time and shouldn't harm the tree as long as the bark is not damaged).

What's in it for the children?

By pushing little fingers into the thick sticky clay mix, children are not only building up their sensory exploration experiences but also building up the hand muscles, wrists and arms which are vital to early coordination and a precursor to early mark making. A fantastic way to explore natural materials both indoors and outside.

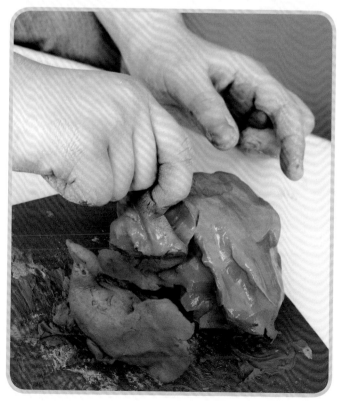

Mud, mud, glorious... clean mud!

What you need:

- **1-2 bars of moisturising soap** (for sensitive skin if possible)
- **Cheese grater**
- **Tray or large washing-up bowl** (cat litter trays make a smaller alternative)
- **1 roll of toilet tissue**
- **Warm water**

What to do:

1. Grate the soap into the tray/bowl.

2. Tear up the toilet tissue into small pieces and add to the tray as you tear.

3. Add small amounts of warm water to the mixture, stirring as you add.

4. Keep mixing until you create a smooth, creamy mixture.

5. Enjoy!

Soap flakes can be used as an alternative to grated soap.

SKIN allergy !

Taking it forward

- Add glitter or sequins.
- Add food colouring or paint to change the colour. (How about a green alien landscape or a blue under the sea world?)
- Add polar animals and enjoy creating snowy adventures.

What's in it for the children?

This is a really tactile messy play experience with all of the texture of mud but without the brown mess! Children can explore using their senses (it smells great!) and use tools and fingers to mark make in the mixture. Also great for stimulating early talk and imaginative play.

Top tip

As with other detergents and soaps try not to get this on the floor as it can become very slippery (even outdoors).

What you need:

- **A new bag of compost**
- **Shallow tray** (gardening gravel tray, builders' tray or cat litter tray)
- **Water**
- **Pots, scoops, spoons, spades, buckets and cups**

Compost is now readily available in supermarkets and garden centres all year round (not just in spring) and can provide a really lovely, unusually textured and earthy smelling material for exploration.

What to do:

1. Open the compost and fill the tray. (Compost should be new to ensure it is mould free.)

2. Encourage children to explore using hands as well as spoons, pots and containers.

3. When children have explored fully, try some of the activities below to extend the excitement.

4. Wherever possible source ecologically sound sources of compost (peat free).

5. After use, make sure children wash their hands thoroughly and recycle compost by digging it into your garden or planters in your outdoor area.

Taking it forward

- Add water to the compost and mix with fingers and spoons. (You can get wooden spoons up to 1 metre long!)

- Hide 'treasure' (gold foil coins filled with card instead of chocolate, old costume jewellery and polished stone gems) in your compost. Provide children with a treasure map for added excitement.

- Bury some dog biscuit bones (or real, cleaned, boiled and prepared wildlife bones) and give children spades and brushes to be paleontologists digging up dinosaur bones!

- Fill a paddling pool with compost and let children physically get into it and dig away (great when you haven't got enough open space to create your own permanent outdoor digging area).

What's in it for the children?

Children not only get the chance to explore a versatile natural material with their hands and feet that feels great and smells really earthy but also build up those essential shoulder, elbow and wrist muscles with all that digging.

Hands on - hands in

What you need:

- **Flat surface** – a table top is ideal (not two tables pushed together as this won't work and you will end up with paint all over the floor), big builders' tray or paddling pool

- **Ready mixed paint in a wide variety of colours**

- **A selection of mark making tools** including sticks, lolly sticks, cotton buds, brushes, dish mops, combs, pine cones etc.

What to do:

1. Squirt blobs and trails of different coloured paints directly onto the table top towards the centre.

2. Encourage children to explore the paint with their fingers, smearing it across the table, making shapes in the paint as they move.

3. Watch as the colours mix together.

4. A relief print of any marks you make can be taken by laying a sheet of paper over the pattern and carefully lifting off.

5. Explore mark making in the paint using brushes, sticks and other materials.

Taking it forward

- Add glitter to the paint for extra sparkle.

- Try scented food essences for a multi sensory experience.

- Add shaving foam to the paint to thicken the mix.

- Try using the paint directly onto a window (make sure you use a window which goes right to the floor so the wall under it doesn't get painted and supervise at all times). Alternatively, you could use a piece of clear Perspex fitted either vertically or laid on the floor.

What's in it for the children?

A great way of making big, over exaggerated sweeping movements with mark making as well as building up finer motor skills essential to early writing.

Top tip ⭐

A squirt of washing-up liquid will help to clean the paint off the table or surface more easily after all the fun is over.

sequins and sparkles

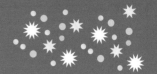

What you need:

- **A selection of different coloured sequins and foil confetti** (readily available from party and pound shops)
- **Shallow trays** (cat litter trays are ideal)
- **Spoons, sieves, pots and scoops**

The availability of seasonal and themed sequins, sparkles and confetti means this activity is not just one for Christmas time but can be themed throughout the year.

What to do:

1. Add a good selection of sequins, and shaped foil confetti to the tray.

2. Explore and enjoy using hands and the tools.

3. Try sieving to see what shapes you are left with.

4. Look for different shapes and colours.

Health & Safety

Remember to supervise as sequins and shapes can get stuck in noses and ears!

Taking it forward

- Try using themed sequins for a starting point for a season talk. (Try Halloween sparkles and plastic creepy crawlies.)

- Mix with other messy play recipes such as jelly (page 30) or porridge goo (page 22) to add another sensory dimension.

- Add sparkles to sand and use sieves to see if you can find the shapes (sieving for treasure).

- Shake some sparkles onto a large horizontal Perspex mirror or a light box and see what shapes and letters you can make.

What's in it for the children?

This is a sparkly dry activity which encourages lots of discussion about shapes and colours as well as offering opportunities for mark making and mathematical language.

Top tip ⭐

A scrunched up ball of double sided tape will help you clean up stray sequins from a carpet.

Frozen fun

What you need:

- **Ice cube trays**
- **Access to a freezer** (unless it's winter, in which case you can leave out over night!)
- **Food colouring – various colours**
- **Glitter**
- **Large shallow trays** (water or builders' trays are ideal) or use a cat litter tray (unused!) for smaller settings
- **Table salt –** in small shakers (old glitter ones are ideal)
- **Jugs for pouring**
- **Access to warm water**
- **Plastic pots of different shapes and sizes** (yoghurt pots, food trays etc)

When playing with ice the tendency is to plan for this kind of activity in winter. This is great and if possible should be offered both indoors and outdoors. However, it is also an activity which can be revisited in the summer, in warm weather, the effects on the ice are much more dramatic and hence children can revisit their experiences and build on them with new observations.

What to do:

1. Make up lots of ice cubes by adding water to the tray and adding a variety of different food colours and/or glitter. (You will need at least 50-100 cubes for good effect.)

2. When frozen, empty out into the tray and explore with fingers.

3. Shake some salt onto your ice cube mountain and see what happens. (The salt will cause the ice cubes to temporarily melt before they refreeze and end up freezing together leaving you with ice cube clumps!)

4. Pour jugs of warm water (coloured with food colouring) over the ice and watch as the colours trickle through the cubes and the warmth of the water helps the ice to melt.

Taking it forward

- Fill trays with different sized and shaped blocks by freezing water in yoghurt pots, food trays etc. By adding food colouring and freezing a part filled pot, then adding another colour and refreezing, you can build rainbow coloured blocks.

- Add objects of interest to the blocks before you freeze them. Small toys that interest the children are great as are coloured shapes and numbers. You can even freeze your own numbers into the ice using stones and other natural materials.

- Make a massive ice block by using a turkey-basting tray in the freezer or even a paddling pool outside overnight in winter. Empty out once frozen and let the children explore the surfaces. Make it even more exciting by freezing treasure such as toys, petals and other objects in the blocks.

What's in it for the children?

This is a great way of exploring first hand the many properties of ice and water and their interrelation. It is a great way of visiting and then revisiting an activity throughout the year. By adding in shapes, colours and numbers the children get to explore loads of mathematical language as they play.

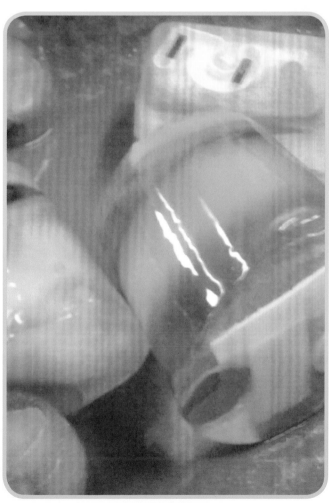

Top tip ★

Make sure you keep an eye on how cold little fingers are getting when exploring ice (especially in winter)!

Icing sugar mix

What you need:

- 1 packet icing sugar
- A bowl
- A jug of water
- Smaller containers or pots
- Food colouring in a variety of colours
- A shallow tray or smooth table top
- **Sticks, combs,** and other objects for manipulating the mix

What to do:

1. Place the icing sugar in a bowl and slowly add water.

2. Mix until you have a thick runny mixture.

3. Divide into smaller pots, one for each colour you require.

4. Add food colouring to each pot and mix until desired colour is achieved.

5. Drizzle the mix into a tray with one colour next to another.

6. Now explore with fingers, sticks, spoons etc and see the colours swirl as you mix them. If you push marks into the icing mix and wait a while it may return to a smooth mix.

7. Leave after playing to allow the icing to harden. Explore again, add some more water and see if you can mix again.

8. Alternatively, drizzle the mixture directly onto the table and explore with combs and sticks, making marks and drawing in the coloured mixes.

FOOD allergy !

Taking it forward

- Use less water to create a dough like mix. Roll and explore as you would with play dough.

- Add food essences such as strawberry, lemon or vanilla to give your mixture a scented aspect.

- Add rice or cereals to give a new texture.

- Try placing some mixture into a cone made from a square of rolled up baking parchment, snip off the end and explore piping the icing into patterns (great for early mark making!).

What's in it for the children?

This activity gives children lots of opportunities to explore colour mixing at the same time as they investigate the changing properties of materials. Adding scents and textures encourages children to use their senses to make sense of their world.

What you need:

- **Dry pasta shapes** — try to ensure you have different sizes (from macaroni to cannelloni tubes) as well as shapes and colours

- **A shallow tray** – builders' tray, gardening gravel tray or cat litter tray

- **A selection of strings of different lengths and thicknesses**

- **A selection of different coloured and widths of ribbons**

- **A selection of pots and pans** (different materials – plastic, metal etc)

- **A selection of spoons and scoops**

- **Sieves, funnels and water play wheels**

What to do:

1. Pour a wide selection of pasta into the tray.

2. Allow the children to explore it.

3. Provide ribbons and strings in case they want to lace and thread the pieces.

4. Scoops and wheels etc are good for pouring and mixing.

Health & Safety. Always make sure strings and ribbons are not long enough to pose a strangulation hazard.

aking it forward

Colour your pasta. Put a small amount of food colouring into a sealable plastic food bag. Add pasta, close the bag and shake to ensure the colour is evenly spread over the pasta. Pour the coloured pasta onto a baking tray and place in the oven on medium heat for about 10 minutes until dry (keep an eye on it as it will burn easily).

What's in it for the children?

This is a great way of exploring familiar materials in an unfamiliar situation. Lots of opportunities to sort and match shapes and sizes and to build hand eye coordination if any threading or lacing occurs.

Crunch, scrunch... lovely leave

What you need:

- **A wide selection of leaves of different shapes, colours and sizes** (collect by hand to ensure they are not soiled and where possible rinse and dry larger leaves with kitchen towel before use).

- **Shallow tray** (builders' tray, gardening gravel tray or unused cat litter tray)

- **Selection of scoops, small spades, buckets, pots and sieves**

Taking it forward

- Make a huge leaf pile on a builders' tray outdoors and hide life-sized animals in it.

- Fill a paddling pool with leaves and let children get in and explore with their whole bodies.

- Put some leaves into the middle of a parachute, large sheet or blanket and work together to see if you can get the leaves up into the air.

- Add leaves to other squishy recipes such as gloop or goo for extra sensory fun (see pages 21 and 22)

Top tip ⭐

Laminate some different coloured, shaped and sized leaves and cut them out so you can carry on exploring leaves all year round.

This is an activity which is ideal for the autumn term, although if leaves are collected and dried in this season, they can be stored in open-topped containers (in a dry place to avoid going moldy) and used at any time throughout the year.

What to do:

1. Place a selection of leaves into a tray.

2. Explore using fingers, scoops, buckets etc.

3. Hide small wildlife figures (hedgehogs, badgers, foxes, squirrels etc) in the leaves and see who you can find. (Small soft toys are excellent for this but remember to wash them after use.)

4. Leave the leaves for a few weeks and keep revisiting – as leaves dry out they will become drier and crunchier.

5. Put trays on the floor and encourage the children to explore the crunchy leaves with bare feet. (Avoid small sticks and twigs that can stick into tiny feet.)

6. When using unwashed leaves make sure children wash their hands thoroughly after use.

Health & Safety

Always collect leaves from a familiar pet-free source

What's in it for the children?

This offers children a great opportunity to interact with nature. Even in settings where outdoor spaces lack trees, it can give children an opportunity to explore natural materials as leaves can easily be collected elsewhere and brought into the setting. This is another example of an activity which is equally suited to exploration indoors and outdoors and which offers lots of variations and opportunities to visit and revisit.

Mashed potato mountains

What you need:

- **Packets of dried mashed potato**
- **Shallow trays or bowls** (new cat litter trays are an ideal size)
- **Warm water**
- **Spoons and whisks**
- **Food colouring**

What to do:

1. Pour the dried mashed potato powder into your tray.
2. Add warm water a little at a time and mix in with spoons, whisks or with fingers.
3. Keep adding water until you have a smooth mashed potato mix.
4. Add food colouring to colour your potato (green, red and purple are all equally impressive!).
5. Pile together to make mountains or volcanoes. Add small plastic characters or dinosaurs for extra interest or just allow children to squish and squash as they please.
6. Dispose of once played with.

Taking it forward

- Add glitter and sequins for a sparkly mash mixture.
- Why not make a dip in the top of your mashed potato mountain, add some bicarbonate of soda powder and then add a mixture of white vinegar and red food colouring to see your mash mountain turn into an erupting volcano!
- Add coloured rice or popcorn kernels for added texture.

What's in it for the children?

As well as providing a starting point for small world play, this mix allows children to squish and squash with their hands whilst building up their muscles in wrists and hands that are essential for early mark making.

Did you know?

At the age of 4 the bones in a boy's hand can be considerably less developed than those of a girl of the same age – worth considering when planning for mark making activities.

Top tip ⭐

Use less water to help form a thicker mixture which can be played with in the same way you would work with play dough mixes.

paste and paper

What you need:

- **A packet of fungicide free cellulose paste**
  (available from all good educational suppliers)
- **Water**
- **Food colourings**
- **A tray**
- **A selection of spoons, scoops and pots**
  (yoghurt pots are ideal)
- **Sieves**
- **Newspaper**

What to do:

Part 1

1. Make up the cellulose paste using the water and following the manufacturer's recommendations.

2. Add food colouring as required.

3. Pour the paste into a tray.

4. Explore using fingers, spoons, sieves and pots

Part 2

1. Make up the cellulose paste as above.

2. Pour the paste into a tray.

3. Add torn up pieces of newspaper to the mix until you have a thick paper mache mix.

4. Explore by squishing, squashing and squeezing.

Health & Safety
Clean up any paste that falls onto the floor as it can make floors and surfaces very slippery.

...aking it forward

Squish large lumps of the paper mix onto thick squares of card, leave to dry and then paint or decorate if desired.

Add food essences to the paste for extra sensory exploration.

Add sequins or glitter for extra sparkle.

Try using a mixture of PVA glue (watered down) and strips of kitchen towel instead of newspaper and paste (much sloppier and extremely sticky but dries clear and very hard!).

What's in it for the children?

Another great multi-sensory activity which, when the paper is added, encourages the squeezing, squashing movements that build strong hand muscles, great for early pencil control. Adding the paper to the mix allows children to explore how materials change and stimulates lots of early science language based around textures and materials.

Let it snow

What you need:

- **Instant snow powder** – available from all good educational suppliers and toy shops as well as online
- **Trays** – gravel trays, cat litter trays, builders' trays, sand/water trays
- **Tapioca** – dried
- **Spoons, scoops, buckets, pots etc.**

What's in it for the children?

Exploring snow in whatever form, gives children lots of sensory experiences and the chance to observe a variety of changes in materials. This is great for building on early science language and understanding and on a big scale for making the most of your outdoor environment.

Top tip ⭐

If you've got space in your freezer why not freeze a big tub of real snow for use later in the year!

What to do:

Snow offers so many possibilities when it comes to sensory play, exploration and stimulating imaginative play and talk. Here are a number of suggestions for ensuring you have snow all year long… not just in winter!

For real

In the event of having the opportunity to explore the real white stuff make sure you get out there and make the most of it before it turns to brown slush! As well as getting outside and just playing in the snow with hands and fingers, why not bring some snow inside in a play tray and let children explore it in the warmth of the indoor setting? Here they will experience first hand the contrasts in warm and cold and see the snow melt as they play. Give children jugs of coloured warm water to add to the snow and watch as it melts. Can they make marks in the snow with the coloured water? Outdoors, use squirty bottles with coloured warm water to squirt patterns into the snow on the ground.

Instant snow

Mix the instant snow according to the manufacturer's instructions. As you mix it together, most artificial snow powders become cold to the touch due to a chemical reaction, hence giving a more authentic snowy sensory experience. Add plastic play figure or polar animals to give children a starting point for imaginative play and talk.

When all else fails...

Empty a packet of dry tapioca into a tray and add some silver and/or white glitter for a winter wonderland experience all year round.

FOOD allergy !

Pitter patter popcorn

What you need:

- **Dry popcorn kernels** (available from most supermarkets)
- **Plastic mixing bowls**
- **Spoons and scoops**
- **Large metal trays** – tea trays or catering food trays are ideal or use baking trays for a more individual approach
- **A selection of containers made of metal** – take away trays, foil food trays, baking tins, tin cans (with edges filed or covered so not sharp), saucepans, etc

What to do:

1. Pour the popcorn kernels into a plastic bowl.

2. Place the large metal tray on the floor.

3. Allow children to explore the popcorn kernels in the bowl with their hands.

4. Now allow children to scoop up some kernels and pour them from as high up as they can onto the trays on the floor. Encourage them to observe the noise as the kernels hit the tray and to see if they bounce or not.

5. Children can explore to see if it makes any difference what height you pour the kernels from.

6. Explore the noise the kernels make in other metal containers.

Taking it forward

- Use dry pasta instead of popcorn kernels – does the sound differ? Why not try rainbow rice (see page 62)?

- Now cook the popcorn kernels according to the directions on the packet and allow children to explore all over again – try filling a big sand/water tray with popped popcorn. Hide objects in it and have fun digging them out.

What's in it for the children?

A wonderful way of children exploring sound as part of a fun play activity. Great for developing early science language and so much more interesting than making a yoghurt pot shaker!

Recycle, re use

What you need:

- **A paper shredder** (a handle powered/wind up model can be used by children under supervision or shred paper away from children prior to the activity using an electric shredder)

- **A selection of different papers** – newspaper, coloured magazines, coloured paper, tissue, white paper etc.

- **A shallow tray** – a builders' tray is ideal as children can climb in to enjoy the activity!

Taking it forward

- Fill a paddling pool with shredded paper and let children crawl around in it.

- Hide toy animals in the paper and encourage the children to find them.

- Use shredded paper of one particular colour as a base for themed imaginative play e.g. blue paper and sea life toys, or black paper and minibeast toys or pink paper and fairy toys.

- Shred foil paper for a shiny experience.

- Add water to shredded paper in large trays outdoors to explore how the paper changes as it gets wet – add some soap flakes to make it even slimier (but be careful as it will also get slippery).

What to do:

This is a nice dry mix great for children who may be reluctant to put their hands in more sticky mixtures. However, do not be fooled into thinking that dry means it's not messy! This is as messy, if not messier, than most of the suggestions in this book so have a vacuum cleaner or brush and pan on hand for afterwards.

1. Shred a wide variety of papers of different colours and textures.

2. Add to the tray.

3. Explore and enjoy.

4. When finished with, it can be added to compost heaps or sent for recycling in the local paper bank.

Top tip ★

This is a great way of recycling some of the materials children may have used in other play activities.

What's in it for the children?

This activity introduces children to the potential of recycling and if themed with toys, can offer a great starting point for imaginative talk and play.

Slime

What you need:

- Cornflour
- A shallow play tray
- Water
- Soap flakes (or grated soap)
- Food colouring

What to do:

Although similar to rainbow gloop (see page 21), this mixture adds an unusual slimy texture which has to be experienced to be appreciated!

1. Add some cornflour to your tray.

2. Add water a little at a time until you create a thick liquid mixture.

3. Add soap flakes to the mixture a little at a time, mixing as you go. (You will probably need equal amounts of soap flakes and cornflour for best results.)

4. Mix until you get a gloopy, slimy mixture.

5. Add colouring and explore using fingers and toes.

6. Add more soap or cornflour to change the consistency of the mixture.

Health & Safety

Never add essential oils to sensory and manipulative play as they can cause serious allergic reactions.

Taking it forward

- Add colours and plastic toys to stimulate imaginative play scenarios – purple slime and aliens are great, as are green slime and minibeasts (toys).

- Add sequins and glitter for added sparkly magic.

- Try on a big scale outdoors in a builders' tray and add leaves, twigs, moss and dinosaurs for an array of play possibilities.

- Add scented food essences or herbs to stimulate the senses even further (strawberry, lemon and orange essences are great or add scented herbs like lavender, lemon balm or curry plant from your outdoor area).

What's in it for the children?

This one really does stimulate the senses and is an unusual variation on a traditional messy play activity hence providing an opportunity to revisit and extend existing learning. Brilliant for stimulating some really unusual and imaginative talk and play, rooted firmly in the children's own interests.

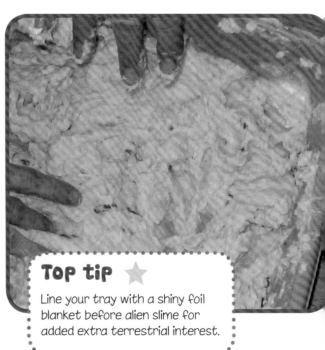

Top tip ⭐

Line your tray with a shiny foil blanket before alien slime for added extra terrestrial interest.

Spooky spaghetti

What you need:

- **Spaghetti** (cooked, drained and cooled)
- **Bowls and spoons**
- **Poster paint in a variety of colours** (red, black, green and orange)
- **Kitchen towel**
- **A selection of small plastic bugs and creatures** (Halloween party packs can be purchased from supermarkets and pound shops and are ideal)
- **Shallow trays** – litter trays or gardening gravel trays are ideal and easily available

Taking it forward

- Make blue spaghetti with plastic sea creatures, shells and starfish or purple spaghetti with glitter and aliens.
- Rainbow spaghetti is always interesting!

What's in it for the children?

A great activity for exploring the properties of familiar materials. An excellent way of combining messy play with small world imaginative play. Great for boosting enthusiasm for talk and storytelling or just for tiny hands to explore.

Top tip ⭐

If the mixture starts to dry out – add a splash of baby oil for extra slippery effect.

What to do:

1. Divide the cooked spaghetti up depending upon how many colours you want.

2. For each colour add a squirt of poster paint and mix in well to cover all of the spaghetti (food colouring can be used but does not give such vibrant colours).

3. Allow the spaghetti to absorb the paint colour (about half an hour should be enough time).

4. Dry off any excess paint by dabbing with kitchen towel (you will not remove all paint and should understand that children will get paint on their hands with this activity).

5. Add the coloured spaghetti to your tray – start with just black and add other colours later.

6. Mix in your plastic bugs and creatures.

7. Let the children loose on the now spooky spaghetti!

8. Dispose of after use.

Shark-infested custard

What you need:

- A tub of instant custard powder
- A large tray – sand/water tray is ideal, a gardening gravel tray works on a smaller scale
- Water
- Spoon for stirring
- Plastic sharks and ocean creatures

What to do:

As custard powder is predominantly made up of cornflour it can be used similarly to cornflour in messy play activities (see Rainbow gloop on page 21).

Uncooked

1. Place some custard powder into the tray and add small amounts of water, mixing as you add it.

2. Stir until you have a paste which is thick enough to pick up in clumps but which when held still will drizzle through your fingers.

3. Add sharks and sea creatures and see where the adventure leads you!

Taking it forward

- Make blue custard and add glitter and sparkles.

- Make custard in jelly moulds, sand buckets and yoghurt pots. Turn out in the tray once it has set and let the children explore the custard castles.

What's in it for the children?

- Great for stimulating talk and storytelling.

- Helps children explore and witness changing materials first hand as part of their ongoing play.

- The uncooked mixture is really good for mark making with fingers and other mark making tools.

What to do:

Cooked

1. Make up large quantities of custard according to manufacturer's directions.

2. Pour into the tray (keeping away from children whilst hot).

3. Allow to cool.

4. Add sharks etc and allow children to explore the cold, jelly-like consistency of the custard. Encourage them to break up the solidified mass as they play.

5. Dispose of after use.

Sparkly tinsel town

What you need:

For each colour:

- Scissors
- **Some lengths of tinsel in different colours, thicknesses and designs**
- **Christmas lamenta in a variety of colours** (available at party shops out of season)
- **A shallow tray –** builders' tray or gardening gravel tray is ideal or a sand/water tray without legs, placed on the floor
- **A large tarpaulin** (it makes tidying up easier!)

What to do:

1. Cut the tinsel into pieces of different lengths (about 2–10cm and never long enough to be a strangulation hazard).

2. Cut up the lamenta so it is separated from its holding seal and falls freely as strands.

3. Put all of the lamenta and tinsel into a tray and place on top of a tarpaulin on the floor.

4. Allow the children to pick up handfuls and let it drop, observing what happens to it as it falls.

5. Be prepared for a fair bit of tinsel throwing and great sparkly excitement!

Taking it forward

- Try filling a builders' tray with the sparkly mix and adding Christmas or fairy figures to stimulate imaginative talk.

- Hide a selection of objects in the tinsel mountain and see how long it takes for the children to find them all. Having a picture treasure list helps.

- Try exploring the tinsel outdoors on a windy day. (Don't use lamenta as you'll never get it back after a big gust of wind.)

What's in it for the children?

An opportunity to explore some real bling as part of their play, with lots of exciting chances to observe the movement of the materials as they are thrown up and fall.

What you need:

- A selection of old used wax crayons
- Pencil sharpeners
- Cheese graters
- Vegetable peelers
- A tray
- An ice cube tray
- Spoons, scoops, sieves, pots etc

What to do:

1. Take the used crayons and depending upon their size, either sharpen them using the pencil sharpener, grate them using the cheese grater or peel bits off using the peeler, until you have a good selection of wax shavings.

2. Place the shavings into the tray and mix up so you have rainbow wax pieces.

3. Explore as you would sand, sawdust, rice etc using the spoons, scoops and sieves.

4. Encourage children to squeeze handfuls of the wax chips together to see them clump up.

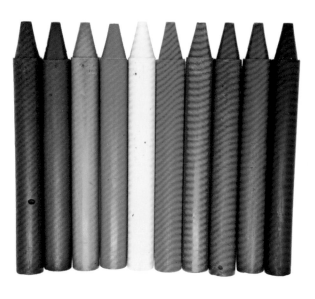

Taking it forward:

- Add glitter to the shavings for extra sparkle.

- Push handfuls of warmed up wax shavings into ice cube trays and chill to make new wax crayon cubes which can be used for drawing and mark making (they have to be compacted quite a bit to ensure they stay together).

- Melt down the wax crayons in an old saucepan and pour into ice cube trays and leave to chill before using (adult activity only – never let children near hot wax).

Try with shavings from coloured pencils that are at the end of their mark making lives for a more wood-based version of this activity – they can be composted after use.

What's in it for the children?

Yet another way of introducing children to the concept of recycling as well as observing first hand how some materials change as they get warm or are squashed. Use your new rainbow crayons to build on mark making skills. The rainbow colours of the wax shavings will promote discussion and the use of language surrounding textures and colours.

What you need:

- 1 large bag of long grain white rice (white rice takes up colour better than brown)
- Sealable plastic food bags
- Food colourings in a wide variety of colours
- A baking tray
- A large tray or bowl
- Spoons, scoops and pots of different sizes, shapes and materials

Top tip ⭐

Have a large-holed sieve available so you can sieve the rice before storing to remove any stray pieces of rubbish or items added in the fullness of play!

What to do:

This is a great dry-mix messy play activity, useful when children are reluctant to interact with some of the more sticky mixtures.

FOOD allergy!

1. Place some rice into a plastic bag.
2. Add food colouring of your choice.
3. Close the bag and squash the rice around in the colouring until it is fully coloured.
4. Empty onto a baking tray.
5. Place in an oven on medium heat for approx 10 minutes until the rice is dry. (Alternatively leave to dry overnight.)
6. Allow to cool.
7. Repeat for other colours.
8. When all colours are complete mix them together into a rainbow mix and add to the play tray ready for exploration.
9. Explore using scoops, spoons, funnels and saucepans.

When finished, seal in an air tight bag or jar until needed next – don't store if the mix has come into contact with liquid as it can go mouldy.

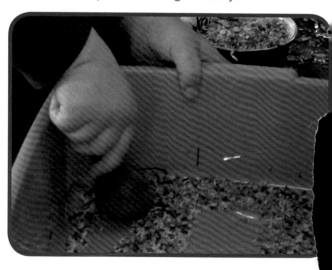

Taking it forward

* Add glitter or sparkles.

* Add different food essences to the rice and dry before use to give scented rainbow rice.

* Try just using one colour of rice (try black or purple) and adding plastic play figures.

* Seal some rainbow rice into a clear plastic bottle with some small objects and see if the children can move the rice around by tipping the bottle to find all the objects.

What's in it for the children?

This dry rice mix has a lovely feel to it and is a real nice sensory experience for children, helping to build those all-important new brain connections. Using spoons and containers of different shapes and sizes can help to improve hand-eye coordination and can lead to lots of mathematical language development including: big, small, empty, more, less etc.

messing with mud

What you need:

- **Shallow tray** – builders' tray is ideal (gardening gravel tray provides a smaller alternative)
- **Mud** – different colours from different sources
- **Water**
- **Selection of tools** – sticks, spoons, brushes, spoons, etc
- **Glitter, washing up liquid, food colouring**

What to do:

1. Place the tray on the floor, on a table top or stand.
2. Place some drier mud into the tray.
3. Explore with fingers and sticks etc.
4. Add water a little at a time... mixing and exploring as you go.
5. Make a really mushy mix and explore with fingers and tools.

Taking it forward

- Add glitter for extra sparkly mud.
- Try colouring your mud with food colouring or paint.
- Try mixing up mud in a big tray on the floor or a paddling pool and exploring with your toes. (You can always make muddy foot prints on paper afterwards!)

What's in it for the children?

This gives children a lovely way of exploring natural materials with their hands (and feet). Using sticks, spoons etc allows them to mark make in a fun and really messy way. Great for indoors and outdoors!

Top tip ⭐

Use warm water to mix... it makes the mud feel even nicer!

50 Fantastic Things to do with Squidgy Stu